21 Days to Joy is a very personal journey to find joy despite the daily challenges of life. Its focus is to move you from moments of doubt into a true sense of joy. This writing will indeed inspire and encourage you to seek the abundant gifts of joy, faith, and peace and will guide you through that process each day.

"Joy is so vital to a fulfilling life. 21 Days to Joy leads us on a wonderful 21-day journey to find joy and incorporate it into the heart as well as everyday life. Never be without joy again!"

> Marilyn Maxwell, M.D.
> Professor of Internal Medicine &
> Pediatrics, St. Louis University

"This writing comes from the heart of a servant of her risen Lord, Jesus Christ. The words will challenge you to examine within and decide your true source. Joy is available to all who desire to be a recipient. If living a life of joy is your desire...this publication is for you."

> Douglass Petty, Ph.D.
> Pastor, Life Coach, Organizational
> Consultant, Motivational Speaker

Copyright © 2008 by Christi Fingal Griffin

U.S. Copyright Office registration #: TXu 1-572-407

Printed in the United States of America

Scripture quotations are paraphrased

Edited by Gloria Ross, Okara Communications

All rights reserved. Written permission must be secured from the publisher to use or reproduce any part of this book, except for brief quotation in critical reviews or articles.

Cover design by Mike Jones, Wisdom Works Inc. and Christi Griffin

C Griffin Publishing, Inc.
PO Box 9331
St. Louis MO 63117

www.ItsAboutJoy.com

Acknowledgments

This book is dedicated to the many people who are the sum total of my life. Without them, I would still be lost. My mother, Caroline Fisher, who brought me into this world, gave me a stellar example to follow and has supported me in every way imaginable. My children, Raina, Carri and David, who have always been the delight of my life, who have grown into exceptional adults and have stood by me through thick and thin. My son-in-law, Alfred, who gives his all to his family and joy to my daughter; my son and son-in-law Keith Jr., whom I affectionately refer to as "my twin"; to my son and daughter Kyle and Khea who challenge both mind and spirit, to my enormously creative brother Mark who inspires me with his belief in my talent; my cousin, Carole Ann, who has prayed for me longer than I can remember; my best friend, Dr. Marilyn Maxwell, who provides as much spiritual advice as medical; my Sister in the Spirit, Lillie, and her friend, Carolyn, who selflessly proofread my writing and encouraged me to take the next step; Rev. Douglass Petty for his wisdom and guidance; to Rev. Earl Nance, Jr. and Rev. Douglass Parham for their support and guidance; Jonell Calloway for her prayers, encouragement, and enlightenment; to my best bud, Archbishop Joseph Naumann, who always exemplifies obedience, excellence and humility; my "little brother", Fr. Maurice Nutt who has faith to spare; Bishop Terry Steib, who has shown me the true meaning of succeeding in the face of odds, to Mike Jones, who has provided invaluable wisdom and direction, and to Keith, my wonderful husband whom I love dearly and who learned to share my joy.

Foreword

One of the latest trends in psychology is the belief that you can change human behaviors by consistently engaging in a different behavior for 21 consecutive days. Through this writing, I thought it time to engage in the process for myself.

For 21 days I made a consistent and focused effort to be joyful "in the midst of every trial." That admonition appears in the Book of James and has always been one of my favorite verses from the Bible: "Consider it all joy, my brother, when you face various trials, for you know the testing of your faith produces patience." James 1:1-3. Those words have guided me through many trying times and attacks of every kind from the enemy.

When Satan sees a weapon of God he attacks and he attacks hard. He leaves no stone unturned in his attempt to steer you away from righteousness and goodness. The attacks are relentless and in moments of physical or emotional exhaustion, he sometimes wins.

Over the last several years, not to mention the entirety of my life, I've been faced with what seems like insurmountable challenges. There have been relentless attacks from every side with an arsenal of weapons usually reserved for the most ardent forces. Through it all my faith has increased tremendously. My joy, however, has risen and fallen like an ocean's tide.

Though not by choice, joyfulness often eluded me. Although I made great effort to maintain a cheerful disposition, the constant demands of everyday life and fierce arrows of attack frequently left me too drained to do so. Sadness and disappointment would creep into small cracks created by the daily pressures of life and little by little my joy was gone. Exhaustion was an open invitation to gloom.

In those moments of exhaustion, the devil would win, strength would be weakened and joy would be stolen. It was then that sinking into depression became a very real possibility and victory seemed a distant dream.

But I've learned that it's at that very moment when joy should be most complete. It's then that you should realize you are doing right, that you are a mighty force for God, that you are a threat to evil. It's then that you should be joyful in knowing that God was, just moments before, comforted by your obedience; that it wasn't He that turned his back to you, but you that turned yours to Him.

I found you can be joyful always when you acknowledge your moment of weakness, when you recognize that it was you and not God who turned away; you become empowered by realizing you can come back and once again accept God's favor. It's in that weakness that you are made strong; your strength is gained from accepting God as the only answer.

And so, it's on that journey that I embark.

8

Table of Contents

Day 1.. 11
Day 2.. 15
Day 3.. 19
Day 4.. 23
Day 5.. 27
Day 6.. 31
Day 7.. 37
Day 8.. 41
Day 9.. 45
Day 10.. 49
Day 11.. 53
Day 12.. 57
Day 13.. 63
Day 14.. 67
Day 15.. 71
Day 16.. 75
Day 17.. 79
Day 18.. 83
Day 19.. 87
Day 20.. 91
Day 21.. 95
Retrospective... 98

"Joy is such a promising prospect. When it can be found, it laughs in the face of loss, disaster and disappointment."

_____

Day 1

The promises of joy

Like so many others, I've allowed the pain from many of life's events to cause me to build a wall of protection. But that wall not only keeps out the pain, it keeps out love and joy as well. It's time for the wall to come down.

Brick by brick the wall was built. Each day invited a new layer. So many years and so many bricks have been stacked one atop another. So how do I tear it down?

If accomplishing this is to succeed, there has to be strong motivation. Years of giving into worldly responses of fear, doubt and sadness is a habit that can be hard to break. When deeply disappointed by the presence of loss, it somehow feels comforting to soothe those feelings with dismay. It's like coating the pain with a sensation different, if not less painful, than the pain of loss itself.

For me, the motivation is simply the desire to be joyful. I've become disillusioned by the promises of melancholy. That emotion leaves a feeling of emptiness and worthlessness. There has to be something more.

Joy is such a promising prospect. When it can be found it laughs in the face of loss, disaster and disappointment. It shakes free the ravaging cost of fear and smiles gently at the invitation to give up.

Reflections:

"By failing to occupy our minds with thoughts of joy, we invite fear, rejection and disappointment to take off their coats and make themselves at home."

Day 2

Joy comes in the morning

Those words are so familiar, so comforting - but that comfort is limited. They suggest the night will bear the pain, that tears will stain our pillow from a heart confounded with grief, that joy has a time clock that sits patiently and waits its turn.

But joy isn't reserved for the morning. It must be found despite the anguish at mid-day, the afternoon disappointment or the evening despair. While joy may come more easily with the gift of a bright morning light, it must also be sought throughout each hour of the day.

Often, the quiet and loneliness of the night

allow still voices to clamor in our heads; voices that constantly remind us of the day's events. But in reality, those voices make their home in the empty spaces we leave by neglect. They can only take up residence when we fail to think on those things that are good and perfect. They can only visit when we leave open a place for them to come and sit awhile.

By failing to occupy our minds with thoughts of joy, we invite fear, rejection and disappointment to take off their coats and make themselves at home. We give them such a warm and open invitation that they can't resist our plea. We make the bed, fluff the pillows and make it far too easy for them to overstay their welcome.

Yes, joy will come in the morning, but only when it's sought throughout the night.

Reflections:

17

"We make great effort to obey those rules set out in the Ten Commandments… But God also commanded that we be joyful - so obedience requires that we are."

Day 3

Joy as obedience

We often think of obedience as avoiding the very occasion of sin. We make great effort to obey those rules set out in the Ten Commandments. We try not to lie, cheat or steal. We banish thoughts of coveting our neighbor's spouse and prepare our tax returns according to the book. We try to honor our parents and to love the Lord our God.

But God also commanded that we be joyful - so obedience requires that we are. We place so much emphasis on those things we shouldn't do, we fail to recognize the things that we should. Rejoice. Be thankful. Give Him praise. Let our hearts be filled with joy.

How much happier we would be, and conscious of His love, if we recognized that God not only wants us to have joy, but that He mandates it. He doesn't just suggest that our hearts be light, but that we make conscious efforts to fill them with joy.

Being obedient is more than going to church on Sunday or doing a good deed for the day. Obedience is fulfilling every word of God. And that includes being joyful even in the midst of the storm.

Reflections:

21

"When we speak words of joy
we not only change our lives,
we change the lives of others."

Day 4

"If you want to change your life, change your words." Author unknown

Those words were written anonymously, but how instructive they are. If our lives are to be changed, we must make conscious efforts to speak words that will change them. We must speak words that are uplifting and full of hope.

Words that we speak go out into the universe. Those words carry on from one person to the next. When we speak words of joy we not only change our lives, we change the lives of others. Words can either build us up or tear us down. They're the balm that can heal a wounded heart and the cure that lifts the downtrodden spirit. And when we lift the spirit of others, we necessarily lift our own.

Words of joy block out thoughts of despair. Our words are our instructions to our hearts. They direct them to abound with hope or to break with pain. They guide them into places of refuge and away from pits of doom. Words of peace and understanding are as plentiful as words of hate and anger. Words of forgiveness and love are spoken as easily as ones of blame and reproach.

Words can wound like a dagger or they can heal like a balm. They can bring hope where none has been and promise where faith has waned.

Words can mean life or death.

Words can bring us joy.

Reflections:

25

" When we make a concerted effort to find joy, we discover it was always there."

———————————————

Day 5

Searching for joy

Day by day, the search for joy becomes easier. It becomes more and more apparent that reasons for joy are plentiful. When we make a concerted effort to find joy, we discover it was always there.

Every day the sun rises and shines its face over the earth. On most days, its light breaks through a cloud-filled sky and inescapably envelopes us with hope. The sun not only gives light but provides promises of a new day. It's the compass that guides us in the belief that new life will spring forth, that warmth will touch our skin - if not our hearts – and that another opportunity comes with the beginning of a new day. How can joy not follow?

If we sit quietly, silence reveals the songs of nearby birds. Joy is in every note they sing. They awaken without care, assured that all they need has already been provided. They need only leave their nests and take flight in pursuit.

Why do we expect less? God tells us He clothed the birds with all they need and that He's counted every hair on our head. The song of every bird, therefore, is a reminder of God's covenant with us - that we are even more valuable.

If we take the time to watch birds fly, we can see the freedom of their flight as they glide effortlessly through the air. It exemplifies a trust we often lack. Without thought or care, birds alight assured they will remain uplifted, that the invisible will keep them in flight. They soar from one space to the next in a ritual of moves that acknowledges God has never failed them. And in all their activity, their joy is evident. Pull up a seat and let their joy be yours.

Without cost or effort we can find joy in all that gives beauty; the verdant grass spattered from place to place, the mist rising above the hills, the shear palate of color displayed in a vast parade of flowers; and the crispness of the air after a cleansing rain. For little more than the effort to open our eyes and minds to the array of nature's gifts, we have joy in packages of every size.

So often we ramble through the day so focused on problems that we fail to see our gifts. We ignore the beauty that freely unfolds as we move from one place to the next. We fail to see hope in budding flowers that break through the hardest ground We fail to take lessons from the most fragile leaf that unfolds at the invitation of light.

Joy beckons us daily. It's offered up in the simplest of things and yet it still eludes us. Joy is always there for the asking; we need only open our eyes and mind.

Reflections:

"Joy escapes us in our everyday life because we've been taught to live in this world rather than in God's."

Day 6

Joy comes in the asking

In our quest for joy we expect to get what we want. We expect that God hears our prayers and that He will answer with rapid speed. In due time, our joy wanes because we believe God has turned a deaf ear. But God has never failed us. Our prayers have never gone unheard. Never. We've only failed to see His answer.

God tells us that we "do not have because we do not ask". According to James 4:2, if we ask we shall receive". And yet, when we ask, we often believe He hasn't answered, because God's timing is not our timing and our way is not His way (Isaiah 55:8).

Like small children, we act as though we've only to

demand what we want and then receive an instant response. We act as if every desire is to be immediately met despite the will of God and the needs of others. We neglect to see that not everything we seek is for our good, nor does it work in concert with the world. And then our joy is gone.

Why then are we told to ask? Why are we promised that we "shall receive"? When we seek to do the will of God, when we desire to walk in love and be obedient to God's word, we soon realize that we already have everything we need. We become open to the abundance that God has already given and we begin to recognize the needs of others. Our prayers then cease to be for what we want but for what gives glory to God.

Did anyone really think those words meant that we could ask for a palace and it would suddenly appear; that we could pray for an expensive car and like the wave of a magic wand it would "poof" into our drive way? Would someone believe that we could only desire a storehouse of cash and expect a bank to open its vaults? How different our world would be if such foolishness took place.

And yet, we do have palaces, our storehouses are filled with abundance, and that car, well maybe a little more effort would produce the result we want.

We simply don't see what we have at our disposal, that we can gain as much pleasure from the enjoyment of everything that's laid before us at no cost as we can gain from ownership. In fact, we can have all the pleasure with none of the expense.

Joy escapes us in our everyday life because we've been taught to live in this world rather than in God's. We've bought into the notion that we must own things, that our worth is measured by what we possess. We forget that in reality everything belongs to God and that nothing belongs to man. We've come to honor the notion of possessiveness and in the process have lost the joy of being.

Like the fable of the boy who could get nothing from the jar because he tried to get too much, we lose the immense pleasure of the princely gifts that surround us by being too busy acquiring the meager trappings that don't.

When we let go of the need to own, the desire to possess, we're able to avail ourselves of the abundance that's already ours as our Father's heirs. We have the time and desire to seek not just our own pleasure but to find pleasure in and for others. And in the process of opening our hand and releasing our greed, we're able to receive all that God intended.

When we take off the blinders of greed, we recognize the magnitude of truly being rich. It's then that we know we've only to ask and only then shall we receive. The answer is always there.

Reflections:

35

"Service nourishes the soul the way food nourishes our body. It's necessary for growth and essential for joy."

Day 7

Joy in serving others

As we busy ourselves on life's journey we often get lost in the trappings of self gratification. We become so wrapped up in our own needs, our own problems, our own desires that we fail to see the needs, problems and desires of others.

Many times wounds caused by the words or acts of one person have been healed by a simple act of another. Small acts of kindness can bring much joy to the lives of others and in turn to our own. They can make all the difference in the world.

Service is the key to a meaningful life. It's the key that opens the door to joy and gratification. It's the road map to peace and contentment.

Formality is never necessary to serve. It may, in fact, shorten the time available to actually make a difference. Service can be as small as extending a smile, waiting a few extra seconds to hold a door for a person on their way or waiting at a stop sign even when you arrived there first. It can take days of planning or just moments of thought.

Service nourishes the soul the way food nourishes the body. It's necessary for growth and essential for joy. It's impossible to have joy within oneself when there's pain left unaided in someone else. It's equally impossible to escape joy when tending the needs of others.

Joy is part and parcel of service. The two go hand in hand. Find someone with a gaping hole in their heart and fill it - someone who is lost and show them the way. Find someone who is injured and heal their wound. The answers aren't in the mysteries of science but in the miracle of love.

Reflections:

"How wonderful to know that joy is ours for the asking. When all else fails, joy takes up the fight."

———————————————

Day 8

The power of joy

There's power in joyful thinking; a power that can allay our fears. It's a power that succumbs to nothing, that summons grace in a moment of need. And it's there; always waiting, always ready to serve. Joy is a very present weapon in the face of despair.

There's nothing that joy can't overcome. Nothing. It's mentioned throughout the Bible in nearly every book, giving light in the face of darkness and hope in the face of fear. Even in those darkest days when the news is more than we can bear, joy can creep in and peel away the pain. But the choice is ours. We can choose to let it in by engulfing our minds with thoughts of joy or we can let it slowly push its way through thoughts of defeat.

When a friend has abandoned us, joy can fill the void. When we've lost hope in the struggle, joy takes up the slack. When we weaken from constant pressure, joy strengthens us. And when our minds are strong, our bodies follow suit.

How wonderful to know that joy is ours for the asking, that when all else has failed, joy takes up the fight. Joy reminds us, "the battle is not yours; it's the Lords." And with that in mind we know we've won before the fight has even begun. There is comfort in knowing that every step of the way is already planned. We need only quiet ourselves and listen to the instructions.

Joy will create the silence we need. It buffers those loud blasts of discontent, those murmurs of pity, and those sad, sad, songs. It shuts out the noise of everyday life, the reminders of yesterday's faults. And in the silence that follows, we'll hear the voice of God and we'll know the battle is won.

Reflections:

"Joy is the most perfect expression of faith. It reflects a complete trust in the promises of God no matter what situation lies ahead."

Day 9

Joy as faith

Joy is the most perfect expression of faith. It reflects a complete trust in the promises of God no matter what situation lies ahead. Even when the enemy is fast on our heels and the Red Sea blocks our path, joy is knowing that God will part the water and create a miraculous escape. Even more so, He'll lure the enemy into His trap and allow the waters to come crashing down. Our safety is assured at the hands of God, our enemies' defeat guaranteed.

With that knowledge, joy can't elude us. In fact, it's the very reason to rejoice. God is watching out. He's got our back. He has gone before us to open the sea and He comes behind us to block the ensuing evil. No harm can come our way when we recognize His mighty hand.

It's sometimes difficult to approach a raging problem, to step forward in anticipation that the sea will be parted and the enemy stopped cold. But faith moves us forward despite the unknown. It's only by faith that we can enter into a realm of uncertainty knowing nothing more than God will see us through. And what joy we feel when victory is won; when we feel God's own joy because we trusted Him as we would want our own children to trust us.

When we face a problem alone we're left to our own devices. We're limited in the strength and weapons we have to use. Our plan of action is no greater than our own wealth of knowledge, our strength no stronger than our last unaided defeat. We're weakened by the enemy's constant attack and our meager efforts to fight back. But when we rely on God's wisdom, God's strength and God's power, we're powerful beyond belief. Who can be against us, if God be for us?

Relying on God in the face of uncertainty is succeeding at the greatest test of faith. It requires letting go of confidence in our own ability and fear of our own weaknesses. Once the false sense of confidence and fear are gone, the door opens to the fullness of God's promises. Joy is the most perfect expression of faith because it's trust in God Himself.

Reflections:

"What we perceive as a problem is no more than God's will waiting to expand our faith."

Day 10

Joy conquers all

Joy conquers all problems. In fact, problems don't exist in the face of joy.

If you define the word problem or look up its definition in a dictionary, you'll find that it's something akin to a disconcerting event that appears to have no solution. The dictionary defines a problem as "any question or matter involving doubt, uncertainty or difficulty". Yet, there is no doubt, uncertainty or difficulty if we face the problem with joy.

Joy invites solutions. It invites everything that is good and perfect. It attracts people who carry the answer we need. It opens our heart to receive the goodness God has promised. It wields strength in its very gentleness. It draws toward us everything we need to win the battle.

Problems can't exist in an atmosphere of joy. Problems thrive on fear and uncertainty, so in the face of joy, problems have no oxygen. And without oxygen, they're deprived of their very life. Gone! Vanished! Poof!

It's very easy to be deceived by a problem. It will disguise itself as bigger than life, and in reality it may be indeed. But in the face of God, problems pale - they simply disappear; sometimes in a flash, other times in slow defeat. It's like watching a balloon slowly deflate until it's small and withered. It no longer bears any resemblance to the enormous ball of air that once floated high above.

Problems are no more than what we make of them. They're contradictions of the perception we had of the way things should be. That's it. No more, no less. We create an idea of what we want and how things should occur and decide that anything to the contrary is wrong. Nothing can be further from the truth.

What we perceive as a problem is no more than God's will waiting for us to expand our faith. The problem was born in the first place because of a lack of faith. When we accept God's will, we cease to have problems. When we are faced with a problem as a result of lacking faith, we have only to increase our faith to remove the problem. Know faith, no problems.

Problems can be made to vanish in an instant, not by magic but by the sheer energy of joy. We need only look a problem in its face and confidently walk away. The battle isn't ours, it's the Lord's.

Reflections:

"Equipped with God's power
and our own
salvation, joy becomes a
natural part of who we are."

Day 11

My joy is my salvation

That one sentence changed my life. It was shared with me by another attorney one day. I would repeat it throughout the day, especially if I felt defeat. For months, though, I couldn't remember if she had said "my joy is my salvation" or "my salvation is my joy". One day, it became apparent that it didn't matter. Either way, joy was the result.

The power in that sentence is the knowledge that no matter what we face, no matter what the circumstances, our salvation in our Lord and Savior transcends all. The earthly things that get in our way, the problems created by man, really don't amount to very much. This world is only temporary and the problems we create for ourselves arise from an ignorance of who we really are: heirs to God's throne, children of the King of kings.

Being saved by Jesus' death on the cross means that we're free of this world's temptations and free of its problems. We're free from the judgment of others and need only worry about the judgment of God. That freedom is boundless. It allows us to walk freely knowing that no man determines our path. It allows us to walk side by side with God, knowing He walks with us, in front of us and behind us. As the poem *"Footprints in the Sand"* tells us, in our worst moments He even picks us up and carries us through the storm.

Our redemption by Christ's blood not only cleanses us of past sin, it gives us the power to avoid present sin. We're released from the need to cheat, lie or steal when we recognize that anything we could gain for ourselves by deceit, pales in comparison to what God has already promised. We're released from a need to gain profit at the expense of others or to hoard that which we could easily share.

Our salvation means our weakness can summon the strength of God. How empowering! At our worst moment we're as powerful as the God we serve. With God, we can face seemingly insurmountable problems and reduce them to rubble. We can whittle away at the greatest obstacle and scale the highest mountain. When we're empowered by our salvation, there's nothing we can't do. In the words of the apostle Paul, "We can do all things through Christ who strengthens us." Phil. 4:13

Equipped with God's power and our own salvation, joy becomes a natural part of who we are.

Reflections:

"It's the joyful heart that prays the most effective prayer."

Day 12

Joy as the only answer

There are small moments in everyday life that can mean more than the most expensive gift. As Easter bid the new day this year, my heart wasn't where it should've been. Indeed, neither was I. In the midst of distress I decided to visit my son at school in Atlanta. It seemed the appropriate thing to do at the time. Not that my problems would not follow me, but the change of scenery and seeing my son would do my heart good.

As I drove the nine hours from one highway to the next, I looked for God in all the surroundings. And there He was at every turn, in every open field, in the pattern of the fallen trees and the blanket of sunlight across the hills. His majesty was evident in the towering mountains, His gentleness in the stagnant streams. He was there for every question I asked, for every tug at my forgetting heart. He was there underneath the wings of the soaring birds and behind the gloom of every cloud.

Just as my emotions went from sadness to joy, the sun glided in and out of the clouds. One minute there was a quiet darkness, the next a shimmering dance of light. And just as intermittent were the ups and downs of my thoughts. It was my thinking I needed to control. It's only day 12 and joy hasn't taken hold in the midst of the storm.

Emotions were reeling, going from the depths of uncertainty to the calmness of hope. And just as quickly as joy would quicken my heart, sadness would wrench it out. Some things are just bigger than others and they require more faith, more faith than you knew you had. It's in those times that God increases our faith.

There are times when just talking to God doesn't seem to be enough, when you yearn to see His face and hold His hand. It's then that He reminds you to seek His face in the face of others. And so I did.

He appeared first in the face of a young woman behind the counter where I stopped for gas. Rather than fume at her inattention, I waited patiently while she finished the page of her magazine before ringing up my sale. Thank God. Before reaching the highway, I realized I was lost. The smiles we exchanged during my first trip inside turned into directions that led me on a most beautiful drive to my destination. A wrong turn had turned into a human exchange and a new direction. But for that mistake, the experiences wouldn't have occurred. Joy was creeping through the cracks in my heart.

On Sunday morning, I noticed what seemed like a brigade of infants in church. Some in mothers' arms, others draped across shoulders. New life offered hope. During communion, I looked intently into the eyes of the homilist as he shared the body of Christ, our eyes expressing the zeal of our risen Savior. He enveloped my hands in an extraordinary gesture of love and added words of blessing. Joy was beginning to take hold.

Standing amidst other Easter Sunday patrons awaiting a noontime meal, a middle aged woman stood to grant her seat to a woman yet her senior. Here in Georgia, where the back door was once the only place the elderly woman would have been welcomed, the Easter spirit gave way to the courtesy of a slave owner's seed. Joy was widespread.

Spending time with my son that day was a reminder of how blessed I've been. From the moment of his birth I knew my son was a gift from God; a perfect angel that made me wonder why God had been so good. And now, we shared a meal, walked the paved roads of Georgia, and recaptured the moments that were quickly passing away.

Yet, back home I knew things hadn't changed. The problems I left would be there when I returned. The same coldness that engulfed me when I departed would await me. In my absence these problems would not change, nor in coming back would they disappear. They would remain throughout the silence and refuse to dissipate without a common prayer. No one person can change a situation created by two and yet God continues to wait until that common prayer is prayed. Where two agree.....

And while God waits, joy remains the answer. It's the joyful heart that prays the most effective prayer.

Reflections:

"When we focus on increasing our faith in God, our minds are turned away from negative circumstances and become fixed on the beauty of His constant gift of love."

Day 13

Joy increases as our faith increases

It's impossible to please God without faith. Just as a parent delights in the trust a child places in those things promised, so much more does God delight in our trust in Him. Children often question their parents about promises made. That lack of trust creates frustration and often disappointment because the child simply didn't believe and trust that the parent's word was as good as gold.

As adults we tend to lack faith in God the same way a child questions a parent's intent. Too often it's not good enough that God has promised to give us more than we could even ask for or imagine, but we destroy the joy that comes in having faith in God and set out to acquire the things we want.

Joy comes in trusting God to bring forth those things that were promised. It comes in having faith that present circumstances don't reflect the coming of His promises. We lose joy in the moment by focusing on the future. Our minds are continually focused not on what we have in our present circumstances but on what we think we're missing. We lack faith in what tomorrow will bring and, as a result, overlook the joy we could experience today.

As we learn to trust in God's promises, we can begin to experience the joy of the present day. We can stop focusing on what we may not have in the future, and simply be grateful for what we have at hand. When we focus on increasing our faith in God, our minds are turned away from negative circumstances and become fixed on the beauty of His constant gift of love. We can take comfort in the knowledge that He is King of Kings and Lord of Lords; that He'll bring us through the rough times and make smooth our path.

As our faith increases, so too does our joy.

Reflections:

"We can glean the joy of the moment or even more so, anticipate a time when a harvest of joy creeps in at an unexpected time."

Day 14

Little acts yield fruits of joy

Little acts can produce an abundance of joy and sometimes the joy may come when least expected.

Several years ago, I planted a magnolia tree outside my bedroom window. It had always been slow in growing and this past year it didn't survive an unseasonable spring frost. It had been interesting to see for the first time, an entire municipality of trees begin to bloom only to be struck down by bitter cold. We were well into May before the tiny green buds began to blossom again and the roadside began to look normal.

I've never taken the beauty of trees and nature for

granted, but this year gave me a particular appreciation for the gift of their boughs.

Glancing out of my window every morning and seeing the dead magnolia, I began to question when (and even if) I would have it cut down. On this particular morning though, my eyes were graced with the beautiful presence of a blue jay perched atop the highest branch. Gazing at its brilliant blue color I realized that planting that tree several years before was now providing a moment of great joy. The sheer splendor and peacefulness of this bird made me realize the power to bring beauty to life simply by such a small act of planting a tree.

It mattered little to the blue jay that the leaves had no life. It didn't matter that the tree's limbs didn't sway in the wind. In its simplicity, all that mattered to this bird was that it had a place to rest and assess the surrounding beauty. It seemed, somehow, that in that moment this little bird and I shared a common place in this world, taking a few moments to enjoy the splendor of God's world; he from the branch of a barren tree and me from my bedroom window.

And so it is with life. We have little more to do than plant a tree, share a kind word, and engage in simple acts of kindness to reap a bountiful harvest of joy. We can glean the joy of the moment or even more so, anticipate a time when a harvest of joy will creep in at an unexpected time. Every moment of each day is an opportunity to plant a seed for the future. Every seed can, in some way, produce good fruit.

Though the blue jay flew away, the joy of that moment remains a present memory.

Reflections:

"If we're to accept the death of Christ as the redemption of our individual sins, we also must accept that He died to redeem the sins of our brothers and sisters as well."

Day 15

Joy in all things

First Thessalonians 5:16-18 tells us to "always be joyful". We are reminded to pray unceasingly and to give thanks in all things because we are experiencing the will of God.

When we were called to recognize our inheritance as children of God and became believers in the redemption of Jesus Christ, we were also called to "suffer" and to bear our cross. The word suffer and the mandate to bear our cross, however, doesn't mean we're to relinquish our joy. Clearly, we've been continually reminded that we're to be joyful in all things. To suffer then, merely means to accept what has come into our lives, and to do so without complaint. When we "bear our cross" we merely recognize that conflict, problems, tragedy and pain are bound to enter our lives. But Jesus died to lift the burden of all our sins – not merely our own but those of others as well.

If we're to accept the death of Christ as the redemption of our individual sins we also must accept that He died to redeem the sins of others as well. While His death empowers each of us to be free of the need to sin, it also empowers us to receive forgiveness when we do. It follows then that if we're forgiven by the blood of our Lord and Savior when we fail to recognize His power over evil, we're also empowered and required to extend forgiveness to others. And when we do, how else can anything but joy follow?

Joy then is always a possibility. When we release sin from our lives and accept our failings and the failings of others, we experience the most perfect expressions of God's love.

Reflections:

"When we live in joy 'always' we know the true peace and protection of God."

Day 16

Joy comes in forgiving; greater joy in forgetting

How often our joy is stolen by the actions of others. Words cut us to the bone, lying steals away our trust, cheating robs us of hope, insults reduce our self esteem. And when we engage in any of the above, we deny ourselves our own dignity.

Whether on the receiving end or the giving end, sin hurts. Wounds are opened and healing takes time. Yet, joy comes in forgiving the wrongs we've committed and the wrongs committed against us. We can choose to hold onto infractions or we can choose to forgive ourselves or someone else and move on in the joy that sin didn't prevail.

Forgiving, however, is only the first step; feeling the greater joy that comes with forgiving requires letting go the very memory of the infraction itself. To hold on to guilt or hurt of our past, even from a moment before, negates that act of forgiveness and robs us of our joy. We can't truly forgive if we haven't forgotten. As the old saying goes, "to forgive is to forget".

We are told to meditate on the word of God, not on the things of our past. Not yesterday, not a few moments ago and certainly not in years gone by. While we rely on the memory of mistakes, hurts and blunders to protect us from harm in the future, the act of doing so increases the chances of recurrence.

When we hold onto the past of what someone else did to harm us, we also hold onto the person we were that allowed that infraction to occur. It's a reality that we attract to us those things upon which we think and focus. If we focus on a perceived wrong, that wrong is destined to recur.

When we fail to live in joy, despite the frailty of those around us, we create fertile ground for tragedy to step in. When we live in joy "always" we know the true peace and protection of God. Joy deflects sin. Joy deflects pain. Joy deflects hurt. Joy is an impenetrable shield that completely protects us from attacks. Not that attacks will cease but that we won't be harmed when they come. Arrows may fly but they can't pierce the armor of joy.

When we accept the forgiveness of our sins, we're released from the burden of that guilt. When we accept forgiveness, however, we're also called to forgive those who have sinned against us. When we're able to forgive the wrongs of others and let go of the memory of their sin, we've truly learned the gift of forgiveness and can live in the greater joy of forgetting.

Reflections:

"It's important then, in the midst of all the burdens we carry, that the spirit we emit to others be one of joy."

Day 17

The spirit of joy

For those of us who live in big cities, we frequently pass one another each day and never even exchange so much as a glance. It's not so much a matter of insensitivity as it is practicality. When we encounter hundreds of people each day, it's difficult to personally acknowledge each one. If we did, there wouldn't be time for thought, for introspection, for conversations with God. As important as interaction may be, personal time is important as well.

That being said, however, even those of us in big cities can't spend our entire lives wrapped in our personal cocoons. Even though we may not notice those we busily pass on the street, ears pressed to a cell phone or eyes glued to a text screen, there's a spirit we emit and a spirit we receive. That spirit can either uplift us or it can pull us down. Our spirit can uplift someone else, or it can pull them down.

It's important then, in the midst of all the burdens we carry, that the spirit we emit to others be one of joy. A smile, even one that's forced, will still beget a smile. Thoughts of good and perfect things bring about feelings that are good and perfect too. When we feel a need to reflect joy in our spirit, we eventually become conscious of the need to actually feel joy.

We're all part of one body - the body of Christ. When one part of the body is hurt, so are the others. When one part of the body is weakened, another part takes over to compensate. If healing never comes, all parts eventually become weakened and worn. We can't experience the true meaning of joy unless all parts of the body are whole.

When we put down our cell phones, step away from our laptops, ignore the mounting e-mails that are forwarded from one person to another, we can find time to actually engage in an interchange of human needs: a look in the eye, a personal greeting and a smile to close the deal.

Even as we pass invisibly through the busiest parts of our day, we can consciously make an effort to feel the joy of God and to let that joy be evident to all.

Reflections:

"Joy can only be found in the moment of being, of feeling and knowing that we're one with Christ."

Day 18

Joy in simplicity

So much in this world teaches us to seek pleasure in outward signs. We bury ourselves in work trying to gain more. We accumulate "things" that give the appearance of success and yet we've failed at one of God's greatest commands: "Be joyful".

As we pile one material possession onto another, we miss the beauty in the simplicity of life. No sooner than we've accomplished one goal, we're off to the next, never savoring the moment of completion and hurrying through the journey ahead. Before the shine has worn from one find, we busily prepare to acquire another; things, stuff, junk. We surround ourselves with trophies of success, reminders that we really aren't that bad.

Yet in all that's gained, in all that's purchased, the joy – if it ever existed – is fleeting at best. Joy is overshadowed by the false sense of worth. It's lost in the relentless pursuit of status, measured by fancy cars, fashionable clothes, exquisite jewels and luxurious homes. Joy eludes the very act of seeking its presence.

Joy can't be found on a store shelf. It doesn't sit idly by with a price tag affixed. Joy is the act of being fulfilled. It isn't in the things we own, the possessions we accumulate or the money we acquire. It can't be found in rising stock values or a savvy acquisition. Joy can only be found in the moment of being - of feeling and knowing that we are one with Christ.

In all that may surround us, lasting joy can only be found in simplicity. And more amazingly, joy is always there, waiting in a quiet place in our heart.

Reflections:

85

"Until we've found joy in those things we can neither collect nor hold, happiness is just a momentary glimpse."

Day 19

Joy in letting go

There are so many things in life that we hold onto: a favorite pair of shoes, pictures from our past, old beliefs. Junk piles up in our attics, our basements and in our minds. We collect things simply for the sake of having them. We clutter our closets with items from our latest shopping trip; we fill our minds with useless information.

Despite the number of things that accumulate in our lives, there's often an absence of happiness. Until we've found joy in those things we can neither collect nor hold, happiness is just a momentary glimpse. Joy isn't found in how much we have but truly in how much we can let go. When we try to cling to someone too tightly, they tend to flee in the other direction. When we grasp a flower too tightly, we crush its beauty in the palm of our hand.

True joy is not in having, but in appreciating. It's found in recognizing that things can't bring lasting joy, only momentary pleasure. In order to have lasting joy we must be willing to let go of those things that only appear to bring pleasure. We have to recognize that possessions bring only fleeting contentment and that our joy is lost in a continuous effort to acquire more, to create more temporary pleasure. We have to recognize that lasting joy isn't found in things but in an appreciation of those things that have deeper meaning.

When we're able to let go of those things that have been given such great importance in our lives, we'll begin to see the many things that had fallen out of focus. We'll be released from the need to continually seek pleasure from things and begin to appreciate the true joy of life itself. We'll begin to smell the scent of a thousand roses, hear the laughter of a grateful child, feel the gentle breeze on our faces, see the smile of a stranger. We'll begin to dine on the true pleasures of life.

When we're able to let go, then joy will be ours.

Reflections:

"The moment we choose to invite joy into our lives, we should begin to treat it as our most welcomed guest."

Day 20

Joy in the order of the day

Joy is always right at our doorsteps, but isn't always seen. It's hidden by the clutter of things and stuff, the negative thoughts floating around in our heads. It's barricaded by piles of newspapers with news no longer relevant, and clothes that no longer fit. It's hidden behind collections of magazines, old bills and broken things that will never get fixed. Joy politely waits until it can emerge quietly, confidently and freely from amidst the disorder in our lives.

Once I realized that joy would continue to elude me until I made room for it to comfortably stay, I began to understand the need to remove the unnecessary "junk" from my closets and destructive thoughts from my head. It immediately became apparent that the two must be done part and parcel. Once we begin the process of preventing negative thoughts from running track in our minds, we feel compelled to create a similar existence in our surroundings. Once we begin to unload the accumulation of things piled up in drawers and behind closed doors, the process creates a similar unloading of negativity in our brains.

The most important part of seeking joy is to make room for it to stay. Joy can be fleeting. If we fail to dislodge old patterns from our thinking and cast reminders of the past from our shelves, it's far too easy for joy to become lost amid the myriad collections of despair.

The moment we choose to invite joy into our lives, we should begin to treat it as our most welcomed guest. Clean out the closets, change the sheets, straighten the pillows, dust the furniture and remove the cobwebs. Cut the dead leaves from plants and add a pot or two of thriving bright flowers. Throw out things we'll never use and donate the clothes we'll never wear. Put out our best dishes and cook up a pot of our happiest memories. Forget the past and make way for the greatest day we've ever had.

… and when we open the door, we should put on our best smile. How else would we welcome our most honored guest?

Reflections:

"When we abandon ourselves and give total praise to God, focus shifts from self to our heavenly Father. We replace our weakness with His strength and see others rather than ourselves."

Day 21

Joy in praise

When all is said and done, the greatest joy comes in praise to our God. It comes in full measure when we thank Him for our salvation, a salvation that comes as sheer grace. It comes without hesitation when gratefulness fills our heart. It comes when we acknowledge the goodness of the Lord.

When we abandon ourselves and give total praise to God, focus shifts from self to our heavenly Father. We replace our weakness with His strength and see others rather than ourselves. Grief subsides, doubt turns to confidence and self pity evolves into compassion.

Joy creeps into even the most rigid heart when we lift our hands in praise and our voices in thanksgiving. Praise cuts through pain, through our deepest grief and our greatest doubt. It forgets wrongdoings, ignores accusations and fights off attacks. It shrugs off insults and laughs in the wake of fear. Praise erupts into joy and joy embraces emptiness with the comfort of God's presence.

Praise is recognition of God's favor. It grants honor where honor is due. Praise is a song that replaces anguish in our hearts and fills hollowness with gratitude. Praise is as simple as a silent acknowledgement or as grand as a shout of halleluiah. It begins with focus on God and ends with a kindled flame that will burn forever.

Praise is perfection of our relationship with God. It joins mere human existence with spiritual awakening. As our voices rise up, so do our souls. We cease to be anchored to the things of this world and emerge cleansed of past sin. We ascend to the heights of our Risen Savior and join Him in the recognition of His glory.

When we give praise to God, joy becomes complete.

Reflections:

Retrospective

Unlike giving up a vice or getting in the habit of exercising, finding and keeping joy doesn't come from just repeating a simple behavior. Finding joy requires a conscious and consistent effort. It demands that we remain in God's presence, that we immerse ourselves in His Word and that we keep His words active in our hearts - for His word is quick and powerful (Heb. 4:12) and when we abide in Him, He abides in us (John 14:4).

We can always busy ourselves with activities that make us happy. Workaholics find pleasure in hours of endless work. Finding joy isn't merely a pleasure and not just a state of being happy. Joy is the very essence of God residing in our souls. It's recognizing His divine Spirit within us and learning to discern His voice.

We may turn our backs on God from time to time, but He never turns His back on us. Though we may be occasionally lured back into states of fear, doubt or melancholy, the joy of God is just a whisper away. He is in the pages of this book, in the depths of our hearts and most assuredly, in the recesses of our minds.

Made in the USA